Creativity and luxury c
ic and industrial hub. A
the interesting mix in
offerings, visible from
galleries to notable arch
clusive exhibitions of some of the most important art collections,
gourmet food and the countless design events give every good
reason for a trip to Milan all year round.

CITIx60: Milan explores the Italian design capital through the eyes
of 60 stars from the city's creative scene. Together, they take you
on a journey through the best in architecture, art spaces, shopping,
cuisine and entertainment. This guide will lead you on an authentic
tour of Milan that gets to the heart of what locals love most about
their city.

Contents

Before You Go

BASIC INFO

Currency
Euro (EUR/€)
Exchange rate: €1 : $1.13

Time zone
GMT +1
DST +2

DST begins at 0200 (local time) on the last Sunday of March and ends at 0300 (local time) on the last Sunday of October.

Dialling
International calling: +39
Citywide: 02

Weather (avg. temperature range)
Spring (Mar-May): 8-19°C / 54-67°F
Summer (Jun-Aug): 18-30°C / 65-85°F
Autumn (Sep-Nov): 10-18°C / 49-66°F
Winter (Dec-Feb): 0-8°C / 33-47°F

USEFUL WEBSITES

Bike sharing service
www.bikemi.com

Public transport news and journey planner
www.atm.it

Citywide free WiFi spots
info.openwifimilano.it

EMERGENCY CALLS

Ambulance/ fire/ police
118/ 115/ 112

Consulates
China   +39 02 5694 106
Japan   +39 02 6241 141
France   +39 02 6559 141
Germany   +39 02 6231 101
UK   +39 02 7230 01
US   +39 02 2903 51

AIRPORT EXPRESS TRANSFER

Malpensa Airport <-> Milano Centrale (Malpensa Express)
Trains / Journey: every 25-55 mins / 52 mins
From Malpensa Airport (T1) – 0543-2243
From Milano Centrale – 0525-2352
One-way: €12 / Return: €18
www.malpensaexpress.it

Linate Airport <-> Piazza San Babila M1 (Urban Line 73)
Trains / Journey: every 10 mins / 45 mins
From Linate Airport – 0060-0107
From Piazza San Babila – 0535-0004
One-way: €1.5
www.atm.it

PUBLIC TRANSPORT IN MILAN

Metro
Tram
Bus
Taxi
Bike

Means of Payment
Cash
Credit card

Single-journey tickets allow unlimited rides on the metro, Trenord rail lines and Passante Ferroviario (Urban Railway Network) for 1.5 hours.

PUBLIC HOLIDAYS

January	1 New Year's Day, 6 Epiphany
April	Easter Monday, 25 Liberation Day
May	1 Labour Day
June	2 Republic Day
August	15 Feast of the Assumption
November	1 All Saints' Day
December	7 Feast of Sant'Ambrogio, 8 Immaculate Conception, 25 Christmas Day, 26 Boxing Day/ St. Stephen's Day

Shops and restaurants are likely to close in the week of and after Feast of the Assumption in August. Shops usually close during public holidays.

FESTIVALS / EVENTS

January
HOMI MILANO (Also in September)
www.homimilano.com

February
Milano Moda Donna (Also in September)
www.milanomodadonna.it

April
Salone Internazionale del Mobile
www.salonemilano.it
MiArt
www.miart.it
Milano Marathon
www.milanomarathon.it
Social Music City (Through to June)
FB: *SocialMusicCityOfficial*

May
TuttoFood
www.tuttofood.it

June
Festa dei Navigli
www.navigliogrande.mi.it

September
Formula One Grand Prix
www.grandprixevents.com/f1-races/italy
Milan Film Festival
www.milanofilmfestival.it

October
SMAU
www.smau.it

December
Fiera degli Oh Bej! Oh Bej!

Event days vary by year. Please check for updates online.

UNUSUAL OUTINGS

Art, technology & stories rooted in the reuse of organic waste
www.theshitmuseum.org

Camping Village Città di Milano
www.campingmilano.it

Vintage Fiat 500 Tour
www.partner.viator.com

Walk Alternative Art Milan
www.waamtours.com

Milan Sunset Photo Tour
www.likealocalguide.com

SMARTPHONE APP

Find bikes & travel log
Bikemi

Journey planner for public transport
ATM Milano

News & updates about the local football club
A.C. Milan

REGULAR EXPENSES

Domestic letters / international airmail
€0.65 /€ 1

Espresso
€ 1

Gratuities
Diners: 10–15% for good service
Hotels: €5 for the porter, €1–2 for cleaners
Licensed Taxis: 5–10%

Count to 10

What makes Milan so special?

Illustrations by Guillaume Kashima aka Funny Fun

Milan has two fascinating faces – the city centre is aristocratic, elegant and historic, juxtaposed against the surrounding districts that have recently been restyled, with the rising of starchitect-designed skyscrapers, cool new restaurants and culture spaces. It's a city to discover step by step. Whether you are on a one-day stopover or a week-long stay, see what Milan's creatives consider essential to see, taste, read and take home from your trip.

1

Architecture

Duomo di Milano
by multiple architects

Fondazione Prada (#13)
by OMA

Complesso abitativo Monte Amiata (Gallaretese II Housing, #6)
by Aldo Rossi & Carlo Aymonino

Museo delle Culture (MUDEC)
by David Chipperfield Architects

Cavallerizze, Museo Nazionale della Scienza e della Tecnologia
restored by Luca Cipelletti

Galleria Vittorio Emanuele II
by Giuseppe Mengoni

Pirelli Tower
by Gio Ponti, Pier Luigi Nervi & Arturo Danusso

2

Milan Staples

Risotto al Salto (Pan-fried risotto)
Trattoria Masuelli, masuellitrattoria.com

Risotto alla Milanese con Ossobuco (Saffron risotto with braised veal shanks)
Al Garghet, www.algarghet.it

Cotoletta (Breaded veal cutlet)
Osteria del Binari, osteriadelbinari.com

Homemade pasta
Pasta Madre, FB: Pastamadre

Pizza
Spontini, www.pizzeriaspontini.it

Mondeghili (Milanese meatball)
L'Osteria da Francesca, dafrancesca.it

Panzerotti (Sweet or savory calzones-like turnovers)
Luini Bakery, www.luini.it

Italian gourmandises & wine
Peck, www.peck.it

3

Classic & Cosy Coffee Haunts

Pasticceria Sissi
Piazza Risorgimento 6, 20129

Bastianello
www.bastianello.com

St. Ambroeus
www.santambroeusmilano.it

G. Cova & C.
www.panettonigcovaec.it

Marchesi
www.pasticceriamarchesi.it

Biffi
biffigalleria.it

Caminadella Dolci
www.caminadelladolci.it

Fioraio Bianchi
www.fioraiobianchicaffe.it

Torrefazione De Pedrina
Via Odoardo Tabacchi 1, 20136

4

Sugar Fix

Panettone (Christmas bread)
Pasticceria Martesana
www.martesanamilano.com

Torta al Cioccolato e Pere (Chocolate & pear cake)
Ranieri, pasticceriaranieri.it

Zabaione (Egg yolks & sweet wine dessert)
Antica Trattoria della Pesa
anticatrattoriadellapesa.com

Budini di Riso (Rice pudding)
Taveggia, www.taveggia.it

Coffee & Sfogliatine di Mele (Apple puff pastry)
Pasticceria Cucchi, pasticceriacucchi.it

Pistacchio Puro Di Bronte
La Bottega del Gelato
labottegadelgelato.it

Chocolate & cakes
Giacomo Pasticceria (#38)

5

Design Museums & Galleries

Studio Museo Achille Castiglioni (#17)
fondazioneachillecastiglioni.it

Museo del Design 1880–1980 (#23)
www.museiitaliani.org

La Triennale di Milano (#14)
www.triennale.org

Museo Poldi Pezzoli
www.museopoldipezzoli.it

Kartellmuseo
www.kartell.com

Armani/Silos
www.armanisilos.com

6

Stay in Style

Beauty & healthcare products
Farmacia Legnani
www.farmacialegnani.com

Century-old hair, beard & Mustache treatment
Antica Barbieria Colla
www.anticabarbieriacollashop.com

Art, fashion & design
10 Corso Como (#25)
Wait and See, *www.waitandsee.it*
WOK Store, *www.wok-store.com*
Frip, *www.frip.it*

Poetic jewellery
Atelier VM, *www.ateliervm.com*
Marina Fossati, *marinafossati.com*

Handmade design
Isoi, *isoi.co*

A perfect Italian-style hat
Cappelleria Melegari,
cappelleriamelegari.com

7

Home Accessories

Designer furniture
Cappellini
www.cappellini.it

Multi branded store
Spotti, *spotti.com*,
Seletti, *seletti.it*,
Cargo&HighTech (#34)

Vintage & Antiques
Spazio 900, *spazio900.com*
Mercatino Penelope,
mercatinopenelope.it
Mauro Bolognesi,
maurobolognesi.com

Sourced by interior designers
Raw, *www.rawmilano.it*

8

Bookshops

A Walther König branch
Armani Libri, FB: Armani libri Koenig

**Design books &
exhibition catelogues**
Bookshop Triennale (#14)

**Fashion books, catalogues &
magazines**
Biblioteca della Moda
www.bibliotecadellamoda.it

**Delicious brioches & cappuccino,
fresh comics, novels, music & art**
Gogol & Company
www.gogolandcompany.com

**Constantly revolving & complete
bookshop experience**
Rizzoli in Galleria
www.rizzolilibri.it/rizzoligalleria

Comics & graphic novels
La Borsa del Fumetto, fumettimilano.it

9

Art Hunt

**L'Ultima Cena (The Last Supper)
by Leonardo da Vinci**
Basilica di Santa Maria
delle Grazie (#8)

L.O.V.E. by Maurizio Cattelan
Piazza degli Affari (#1)

**Mini-monuments by the likes of
Lucio Fontana and Adolfo Wildt**
Cimitero Monumentale (#11)

Via Dolorosa by Mark Wallinger
Crypt of Duomo di Milano

The Path by Bill Viola
Chiesa di San Marco

**Trompe-l'oeil apse
by Donato Bramante**
Chiesa di Santa Maria presso
San Satiro (#9)

Provocative work by young artists
The vitrine outside Il Carpaccio
Via Lazzaro Palazzi 19, 20124

10

Culture
& Leisure

A walk at Sunset
Roof of Duomo di Milano,
Vivaio Sorelle Riva
Via arena 7, 20123

Watch a puppet show
Teatro Colla
www.teatrocolla.org

Opera & music
Teatro alla Scala
www.teatroallascala.org

**Bike along Naviglio della
Martesana, have lunch at
Cassano d'Adda village or picnic
on the way**

**Have Aperitivo zucca at the
bar desk of Camparino, Galleria
Vittorio Emanuele II or in Navigli,
6–10pm**

Icon Index

 Opening hours   Admission

 Address   Facebook

 Contact   Website

 Remarks

 Scan QR codes to access Google Maps and discover the area around each destination. Internet connection required.

60x60

60 Local Creatives x 60 Hotspots

From vast cityscapes to the tiniest glimpses of everyday exchange, there is much to provoke one's imagination. 60x60 points you to 60 haunts where 60 arbiters of taste develop their good taste.

Landmarks & Architecture

SPOTS · 01 – 12 📍

Milan's skyline has a huge mix of styles, shapes and atmospheres, but quite well divided in areas, so that you won't get lost and can find your favourite one to fix your gaze upon.

Cultural & Art Spaces

SPOTS · 13 – 24 📍

From big institutional places to small and avant-garde cinemas, art galleries and theatres, the city's great and international creative panorama will satisfy every cultural taste.

Markets & Shops

SPOTS · 25 – 36 📍

Milan is one of the world's most renowned fashion capitals, but designer wear is not the only thing to fill your bag. Don't fly away without local curiosities and vintage finds.

Restaurants & Cafés

SPOTS · 37 – 48 📍

Italy's best culinary tradition concentrates in Milan, so plan your diet after the trip! Start the day with a cappuccino, then sample regional and national recipes in new and classic ways.

Nightlife

SPOTS · 49 – 60 📍

Although its nightly fancy parties, pubs, cinemas and theatres draw a cool crowd, Milanese best-loved way to spend the night is to simply talk to a friend with a beer in hand.

Piazza degli Affari e L.O.V.E. @ P.014

Landmarks & Architecture

Storied heritage, experimental endeavours and district-wide renewal

Milan's history dates back to the ancient Roman Empire and it's visible everywhere if you look close enough. While majestic structures like Duomo di Milano are hard to miss, try spotting the humble entrance to the Santa Maria presso San Satiro church (#9) between bustling apparel chain stores and uncover one of the world's first trompe l'œil attempt there; or glance up at the arching glass ceiling, built in 1865, when you shop at Galleria Vittorio Emanuele II.

Around the 1950s, Milan's modern identity emerged through the rise of experimental architectural projects. Foreword-thinking minds were not afraid to try out new styles and materials while fulfilling increasing demand for commercial and living spaces in the post-war period. The results are structures like Velasca Tower (#2) by BBPR and Pirelli Tower by Gio Ponti, both still stand proud today.

Redevelopment projects in recent years give distinctive new looks to various districts that mark Milan's rich industrial past. From Norman Foster's Milano Santa Giulia green residential plan, to the Porta Nuova business district by the likes of Cesar Pelli and Stefano Boeri, cutting-edge constructions and thoroughly-planned greenery juxtaposed against the well-preserved historic gems to show the constant reinvention of Milan – a city respectful of its heritage, while driving design forward on its terrain.

Diego Grandi
Founder & designer, DGO

Milan adopted me where I research on the codes of contemporary living and depth of surface as a trained architect. My specialties are product, interior and exhibition design.

Torre Velasca
P.015

Nicola Ricciardi
Independent curator

Having lived in Berlin and New York, I'm happy to be home where I curate for private and public art institutions. I also write art critique for Mousse, Frieze and The Brooklyn Rail.

Arthur Arbesser
Creative director, Iceberg

Originally from Vienna, I joined Giorgio Armani's design team in Milan after studying at Central St. Martins. I also run my own label and presented my first collection at Milan Fashion Week in 2013.

Piazza degli Affari e L.O.V.E.
P.014

Castello Sforzesco
P.016

Damiano Spelta
Furniture designer

I call myself an art-designer. It seems that my mission is to create emotions and I feel my biggest emotion when I see people observe my works and smile. Have a nice trip.

Casa Rustici
P.018

Studio Pepe
Design agency

Set up by Arianna Lelli Mami and Chiara di Pinto in 2006, Studio Pepe takes an all-round approach to interiors and product design and runs as a creative consultancy in all its forms.

Marco Klefisch
Visual artist

I work in the field of creative direction, set design, illustration and create experimental contents for events and fashion shows. I hate taxonomy in my profession. I believe in words.

Piazza Gae Aulenti
P.017

Complesso abitativo Monte Amiata
P.019

Lady Tarin
Photography

I'm an Italian artist and a Fine Arts Academy of Bologna graduate. My work feeds on my fashion works as fashion feeds my personal research that investigate eroticism as a life force.

Basilica di Santa Maria delle Grazie P.022

Goldschmied & Chiari
Artist duo

Sara Goldschmied and Eleonora Chiari creates with photography, video and installation. They were winners of the Castello di Rivoli Museum prize for best Italian young artists in 2012.

Enrico Pompili
Creative director & set designer

I design sets with Valentina Cameranesi for international magazines and companies. I adore books and I treasure the atmosphere of my area, Porta Venezia / Risorgimento.

Villa Necchi Campiglio P.020

Chiesa di Santa Maria presso San Satiro P.023

Umberto Angelini
Founder & artistic director, Uovo

Uovo is an independent organisation in Milan which realises festivals and events around contemporary creativity. I'm also the general manager of Teatro Grande.

Cimitero Monumentale P.025

Nicolas Bellavance-Lecompte, *Creative consultant*

Born in Montreal, Bellavance-Lecompte now lives between Milan and Beirut. He co-founded design studio Oeuffice and Carwan Gallery, gives advice to various and curates exhibitions.

Matteo Morelli
Graphic designer & illustrator

Raised in Milan, Matteo Morelli has a strong passion for antiquities and oddities. His work aims to take the elegant 19th-century aesthetics into the contemporary and digital design era.

Chiesa di San Bernardino alle Ossa P.024

Brera P.026

1 Piazza degli Affari e L.O.V.E.
Map C, P.102

Piazza degli Affari serves as a symbol of the Italian economy as the headquarter of the Italian Stock Exchange since the beginning of the 20th century. The economic crisis in 2010 gave way to the provocative artist Maurizio Cattelan who was granted permission to temporarily show his sculpture L.O.V.E. in the square. The 11 metres high hand in marble with just the middle finger showing, is said to express irreverence against the financial world and the fascist architecture of the Stock Exchange. Disapprovals and eulogies followed its imminent removal, awarding the sculpture global fame and the city made concession to keep it.

🏠 *Piazza degli Affari, 20123*

"Go there by night when the atmosphere is suspended, almost in a metaphysical state."

– Diego Grandi, DGO

2 Torre Velasca

Map C, P.103

Unique in its shape, and standing 100 metres tall, the Velasca Tower defines the city's skyline. Loved and hated from its inception, its "mushroom" silhouette is designed to resemble Renaissance watchtowers blending in with the classic architecture in the historic district. Designed in the 1950s by BBPR, it became one of the symbols of modern Milan and was re-styled by Piero Lissoni for EXPO Milano 2015, while maintaining its brutalist features. Emphasising multifunctionality, the lower floors of the tower hosts shop and offices, while the airier top floors are residential units with panoramic view. A new exhibition area also opens to the public for design shows and talks.

🏠 *Piazza Velasca 3-5, 20122*
URL *www.urbanupunipol.com/ torrevelasca*

"It's been a Milanese landmark that stands out with its unique shape and size since the 1950s."

– Arthur Arbesser, Iceberg

3 Castello Sforzesco
Map C, P.102

Once home to the Sforza family who ruled Renaissance Milan, this majestic red brick structure was built in the 14th century as a fortress and later expanded and graced by the works of artistic talents of the time. Admire Leonardo Da Vinci's fresco at the Sala delle Asse and get in touch with his legacy through this ancient space he helped to fortify. Set eyes on Michelangelo's last masterpiece Pietà Rondanini at one of the seven cultural and art museums within the castle, alongside some of the most important Italian paintings at the gallery. The tumultuous history of the castle is evident in battlements, ravelins and other castle defences, which are brought close to their original appearance by modern restoration efforts.

🕐 0700-1930 daily, Museum: 0900-1730 (Tu-Su, except Jan 1, May 1 & Dec 25) 💲 Museum: €5/3/free admission after 1400 (Tu), 1630 (W-Su) & monthly first Sundays (Nov-Jul)
🏠 Piazza Castello, 20121
🔲 www.milanocastello.it

"It's the one and only place you should visit if you have less than 24 hours in town. Make sure to stop by the new Pietà Rondanini Museum to view Michelangelo's last sculpture." – Nicola Ricciardi

4 Piazza Gae Aulenti
Map F, P.106

Dedicated to the late Italian architect Gae Aulenti, this AECOM-developed public square amidst the bustling Porta Nuova Garibaldi commercial area oozes tranquility. A key element of an urban renewal project that defines cosmopolitan Milan, the square features a streamlined pool with three oval cascades that draw light and air down to the retail floor and car park below. Loosen up on the seating areas that stretch around the pool, let the sound of flowing water offset hectic noises and admire the encircling city life in reflection. The square is highly accessible from other parts of town, you may also visit the award-winning Bosco Verticale through one of the elevated walkways.

🏠 *Piazza Gae Aulenti, 20100*

"It's the new architect jewel for the Milanese."

– Damiano Spelta

5 Casa Rustici
Map J, P.108

Designed by renowned architects Giuseppe Terragni and Pietro Lingeri in the 1930s, this rationalist residential building became a prominent prototype for modern housing design in Milan. The six-storey structure features two parallel blocks connected by open-air walkways above ground level, allowing ample light into the spacious courtyard in between. By increasing structural transparency and eliminating the traditionally enclosed courtyard, the approach breathed new life to the design of public space. The rooftop penthouse was occupied by Vittorio Rustici, then owner of the building, surrounded and hidden by trees and plants as it was a normal house with a garden.

🏠 *Corso Sempione 36, 20154*

"*Watch La Notte (1961) directed by Michelangelo Antonioni for a good glimpse of Milan's modern face and architecture in the early 1950s before your visit!*"

– Studio Pepe

6 Complesso abitativo Monte Amiata

Map S, P.111

Off the beaten track find this outlandish residential complex designed in the 1960s by two prolific Italian architects, Carlo Aymonino and Aldo Rossi. The shape of the building clashes with its surroundings, with five buildings at different heights and depths, all linked together by fluorescent corridors, spiral staircases and void public areas on the ground level hold up by lofty columns and slabs. Walking into the complex, one feels like immersing into a Surrealist painting by Giorgio de Chirico. The geometry of the buildings serves as an icon for new generations of creatives.

🏠 *Via Enrico Falck 53, 20151*

"It's a brilliant example of a well-thought architecture off the city's centre."

– Marco Klefisch

7 Villa Necchi Campiglio
Map D, P.104

Hidden in an idyllic garden in Milan's city centre, Villa Necchi Campiglio is a cultural and architectural jewel designed in the 1930s by Piero Portaluppi for the Necchi Campiglio family, industrialists known for the invention of Necchi sewing machine. Today it's a house-museum owned by the Italian National Trust and aims to re-introduce Portaluppi's work to the public. Addressing practicality in space planning and completed with advanced amenities of the time such as an intercom system and Milan's first heated swimming pool, the villa oozes modernity and represents the understated grace of Milanese bourgeoisie in that era. The villa was used for the set of the film *I Am Love* (2009) starring Tilda Swinton and directed by Luca Guadagnino.

🕐 1000–1800 (W–Su), By guided tour only 🆂 €10/5/4
🏠 Via Mozart 14, 20122
☎ +39 02 7634 0121
🔗 www.visitfai.it/villanecchi

"Make a reservation for their guided tours!"
– Lady Tarin

8 Basilica di Santa Maria delle Grazie

Map B, P.102

Listed as one of UNESCO's world heritage sites, this complex of church and sanctuary is renowned worldwide as home to *The Last Supper* by Leonardo Da Vinci in its refectory. The famous painting was originally created with experimental paints and over time began to deteriorate. In 1999, after years of restoration, the grand unveiling of the original chromatic palette of the masterpiece took place. Due to its fragility, visitors are divided in small groups and, considering the huge number of visits daily, it's recommended to make a booking two months in advance by phone or online.

🕐 M-F: 0700–1200, 1530–1930 (winter only), 0700–1200, 1600–1930 (summer only), P.H.: 0730–1230, 1600–2100
🏠 Piazza di Santa Maria delle Grazie, 20123 URL legraziemilano.it
🎟 The Last Supper tour: €12/7, advance booking required, +39 02 9280 0360, www.vivaticket. it/?op=cenacoloVinciano

"It's the most beautiful church in Milan!"

– Goldschmied & Chiari

9 Chiesa di Santa Maria presso San Satiro

Map C, P.103

Built on an ancient shrine of St. Satyrus for over a millennium, the church was later dedicated to St. Mary as well. It is known for a defining feature – a false apse that fills the space with one of the first examples of trompe l'oeil in artistic history – and is considered an eminent work of the Italian Renaissance. The ornate interior features frescoes and intricate designs of biblical scenes giving this sacred space an aura of glory in its past and present. The Neo–Renaissance facade of the church is often missed by visitors as it's hidden off the main road in between boutiques and shops.

🕑 0730–1130, 1530–1900 daily
🏠 Via Torino 19, 20123

"It's especially spectacular when the light permeates the clerestory windows and hits the columns like Nordic light."

– Enrico Pompili

10 Chiesa di San Bernardino alle Ossa

Map C, P.103

Fascinating, unique, even macabre for some, San Bernardino alle Ossa is best known for its ossuary. It all started in 1210 when a chamber was built adjacent to a cemetery to accommodate its human skulls and bones, and the church came later in 1269. Together with victims of plague from the ancient Brolo Hospital and other local graveyards, the bones were meticulously arranged to bedeck the walls, pillars and doors of the ossuary during different phases of reconstruction between 17th and 18th century. Set off by a fresco of flying angels by Sebastiano Ricci, this solemn interior is a reminder of Milan in the 1600s, a dark period in time of pestilences and shortage.

🕐 0900–1200, 1300–1800 (M–F), 0730–1230 (Sa), 0900–1200 (Su)
🏠 Via Verziere 2, 20122

"Let yourself be enchanted by its unsettling beauty in a magical and astonishing atmosphere."

– Umberto Angelini, Uovo

11 Cimitero Monumentale
Map O, P.110

A walk through Monumental Cemetery will take you through Who's Who in Milan's history. The beautiful burial ground enshrines the graves of arguably the richest or most influential Milanese from the 19th century onwards, such as conductor Arturo Toscanini and novelist Alessandro Manzoni. The graves are real masterpieces that reflect the Italian history of art. Take a walk through time amidst murals, bronzes, obelisks, temples and sculptures constructed in the age of Realism, to the Art Nouveau of the early 20th century and the later period of modernism, it's a real museum en plein air. You can get information about the cemetery as well as other ongoing cultural events in the city at the Infopoint at the entrance.

 ⏰ *0800–1800 (Tu–Su), –1300 (Jan 1, Easter Su & M, May 1, Jun 2, Aug 15, Dec 8, 25–26)* 🏠 *Piazzale Cimitero Monumentale, 20154* ☎ *+39 02 8846 5600* 🖉 *90 mins free guided tour (IT/EN): Booking required, dsc.visiteguidatemonumentale@comune.milano.it, +39 02 8844 1274*

"Do not miss the curious pyramidic funerary shrines."

– Nicolas Bellavance-Lecompte

 Brera
Map C, P.103

Brera is at the creative heart of the city, full of artistic history both in the built environment and inside the many galleries, one of them Pinacoteca di Brera, that houses works from the Renaissance period to current times. Apart from Accademia delle Belle Arti di Brera, an acclaimed fine arts academy that has been around since 1776, you'll also find an observatory and a botanical garden in the area. Stroll along the cobblestone streets and admire the amalgamation of Baroque style columns and Neoclassical-designed squares all melding into a harmonious urban landscape. Today Brera is also a design district, with showrooms of leading brands such as Moroso and Fritz Hansen, as well as numerous designs studios.

 Brera, 20121

 "Start from Duomo and head to Garibaldi, the skyscraper district, and you will see how the city evolves through time."
– Matteo Morelli

Fondazione Prada, P.032

Cultural & Art Spaces

Boutique galleries, starchitect-designed museums and creative space conversions

Milan has an extensive cultural offering, fusing the past and present through space and form. The city's manifold industrial background leaves behind huge open structures. The success of creatives' and artists' self-initiated revamp efforts encouraged larger scale commissions by the local government as well as cultural institutions. Pirelli HangarBicocca (#24) inside the former factory of high power machinery and Fondazione Prada (#13), a distillery from the early 1900s re-designed by OMA are two of many sites that have been transformed into multidisciplinary spaces. Housing international exhibitions, performances, movie screenings and forums, the buildings' heritage lives on by becoming part of Milan's vibrant cultural happenings. Apart from colossal spaces, Milan also has pockets of small galleries and theatres dotted all over its territory. La Triennale di Milano (#14) and the Teatro Franco Parenti (#20) are perfect places to embrace the experimental nature of a new wave of world-class exhibitions and productions in town. Of course, no visit to Milan is complete without a glimpse of an original Leonardo da Vinci. Make a booking to experience *The Last Supper* with your own eyes at Basilica di Santa Maria delle Grazie (#8), or visit the Biblioteca Ambrosiana for a close look at the great master's Codex Atlanticus notebooks.

Narguess Hatami
Fashion designer, Miahatami

I'm a fashion designer from Israel. I lived in Tehran until I moved to Italy because of the love for my job. Miahatami is a multicultural brand where West meets the real Persian tradition.

La Triennale di Milano
P.034

Thomas De Falco
Textile artist

Thomas De Falco's work takes its origins from ancient tapestry weaving techniques. His art is based on performances, where candid bodies interlink, covered by textile stripes.

Massimo Torrigiani
Co-founder, Boiler Corporation

Torrigiani also co-founded Fantom, a curatorial collective dedicated to photography and the visual arts. He has been the creative director of Art In The City Shanghai since 2014.

Fondazione Prada
P.032

Padiglione d'Arte Con- temporanea
P.035

Ugo La Pietra
Architect, artist, editor & teacher

A theorist of disequilibrating design, La Pietra re-investigates relationships between design and crafts. In 2014, a retrospective at La Triennale reviewed his work backdated to 1960.

Studio Museo Achille Castiglioni
P.038

dotdotdot
Multidisciplinary design studio

Set up by Alessandro Masserdotti, Giovanna Gardi, Laura Dellamotta and Fabrizio Pignoloni, we are a team of philosophers, engineers and designers who melds architecture with media technology.

Chiara Mirelli
Photographer

Music is a part of my life besides photography. I have been shooting portraits, booklets, video clip and reportage on Italian artists from every genre. LUZphoto distributes my photo archive.

Museo del Novecento
P.036

Micamera
P.039

Stefania Beltrame & Paolo Bazzani, *Creative duo*

Art director Paolo Bazzani and architect Stefania Beltrame often land on the same projects around fashion. They became Milaneses during the years and they like this city.

Teatro Franco Parenti
P.041

Laura Lamonea
Art director, Video Sound Art

I am particularly drawn to the theatrical elements in visual art. I art-direct Video Sound Art festival which champions creative concoction and technological innovation in the arts.

Marco Pozzi
Graphic design studio

Marco Pozzi has been part of the Ipotesi Cinema movement and taught TV direction at the IULM University of Milan. He also directed ads for Valentino and Coca-Cola, films and sit-coms.

Galleria l'Affiche
P.040

Anteo spazioCinema
P.042

LaTigre
Creative consultancy

Founded by Luisa Milani and Walter Molteni, LaTigre specialises in visual solutions and data visualisation. We use a contemporary language grounded in a love of the classics.

Museo del Design
1880–1980
P.044

Alberto Biagetti & Laura Baldassari, *Designer-artist duo*

We create unique objects for the homes of the past and the future. Our project explores the complexities of space where aesthetics and functionality are accented by surprises.

Paolo Santambrogio
Fashion photographer & director

I'm 100% Milanese (my last name guarantees it) and I'm very proud to be a Milanese and an Italian. In my work fashion and aesthetics are not an end in itself but the start of a broad narrative path.

Cinema Beltrade
P.043

Pirelli HangarBicocca
P.046

13 Fondazione Prada
Map H, P.107

Built in the early 20th century, this former 19,000-square-metre gin distillery became Fondazione Prada's permanent home after an eight-year renovation. Using elements of the space to convey meaning, starchitect Rem Koolhaas of OMA placed emphasis on openness with the design. Modernised structures and iconic buildings intertwine where Miuccia Prada's own art collections, screenings and temporary exhibits collide. For a surreal experience, visit the public hangout, Bar Luce, designed by the film director Wes Anderson and akin to a movie set.

🕐 1000-2000 (M, W-Th), -2100 (F-Su)
💲 €10/8 🏠 Largo Isarco 2, 20139
☎ +39 02 5666 2611
🌐 www.fondazioneprada.org
✎ Guided tours: €80 for 1-25 pax,
2-day (IT/EN) and 1-week (FR/DE/ES)
advance booking required

"It's more a space that brings you to another dimension. Don't forget to also see the bar."

– Narguess Hatami, Miahatami

14 La Triennale di Milano
Map A, P.102

Regarded as Milan's hallmark of Italian design, La Triennale di Milano is a showcase of the best in art, design, architecture, fashion and crafts-manship. Inside the impressive Rationalist Palazzo dell'Arte designed by Giovanni Muzio in 1933 is the museum that welcomes visitors all year round with permanent collections of the triennial as well as an eclectic mix of objects, expertly curated. Giorgio de Chirico's Fountain of Mysterious Baths, designed for the 1973 triennial is in the garden, and worth a visit. The outdoor café has an impressive large crystal glass window perfect for people-watching whilst drinking a coffee.

🕐 1030-2030 (Tu-Su) 💲 €15/12/4
🏠 Palazzo della Triennale, Viale Alemagna 6, 20121 📞 +39 02 724 341
URL www.triennale.org

"I had my first performance there so I love this place. Head to the terrace of the exhibition room on the first floor to admire the panorama."

– Thomas De Falco

15 PAC
Map D, P.104

Padiglione d'Arte Contemporanea (PAC) is a contemporary art space hosting international artists such as Marina Abramovic, Vanessa Beecroft and Tony Oursler. The building is a masterpiece of Italian modernism, designed by Ignazio Gardella and opened in 1954. Terribly destroyed in an attack by the Mafia in 1993 for being a symbol of the Italian culture, it was rebuilt nearly identically in 1996 by Gardella. PAC is next to the Galleria d'Arte Moderna, also worthy to be seen.

🕓 0930–1930 (Tu–W, F–Su), –2230 (Th)
💲 €10/5 (Th, after 1930)
🏠 Via Palestro 14, 20122
📞 +39 02 8844 6359
🔗 www.pacmilano.it
📎 Free guided tours: 1900 (Th), 1730 (Su)

"Go during the week when there are less people."

– Massimo Torrigiani, Boiler Corporation

16 **Museo del Novecento**
Map C, P.103

Next to Duomo di Milano, the Museo del Novecento is inside the Mussolini-era Arengario Palace, a remarkable complex in its own right. Enter from a large lobby on the ground floor through a subway, and a large spiral ramp leads you straight to its expansive 20th century Italian art collection, with Pelizza da Volpedo's Il Quarto Stato symbolically marking the start of an era of great social and political change. End your visit with a trip to the terrace for panoramic views overlooking the Duomo.

🕐 0930–1930 (Tu–W, F, Su), 1430– (M), –2230 (Th, Sa)
💲 €5/3/free admission (M, W–Su: 2hrs before closing, Tu: 1400–) 🏠 Via Marconi 1, 20123
📞 +39 02 8844 4061
🔲 www.museodelnovecento.org
🔗 Guided tour (EN/FR/ES/DE): Advance booking required, +39 02 6597 728, info@adartem.it

"*This is a place with a very strong cultural identity.*"
– Ugo La Pietra

17 Studio Museo Achille Castiglioni

Map A, P.102

Achille Castiglioni (1918–2002) spent half his life testing wild ideas, creating design classics like the Arco floor lamp and Mezzadro stool. Now a foundation run by his family, the public can wander through the design master's studio exploring original sketches, prototypes and designs. Giovanna, his daughter is the source of many anecdotes during the hour-long tour. The studio-museum is currently a self-sustaining project, so donations and patron visits help keep its doors open.

🕐 By guided tours only: 1000, 1100, 1200 (Tu-W, F), 1830, 1930, 2030 (Th), max 20 pax or min 15 (Sa), by email appointment only 💲 €10/7 🏠 Piazza Castello 27, 20121 📞 +39 02 8053 606, info@achillecastiglioni.it 🔗 fondazioneachillecastiglioni.it

"It's the place we love. Book a guided visit with Achille Castiglioni's daughter for a total immersion in the project and in the normality of a genius."

– dotdotdot

18 Micamera

Map K, P.109

Both a photography bookstore and a gallery, Micamera occupies a small place in the middle of the young and bohémien Isola district. Despite its small geographic presence, it's the biggest online photography bookstore in Italy, selling rare and limited editions at affordable prices. Micamera is owned by husband and wife duo Flavio Franzoni and Giulia Zorzi who organise exhibitions, books launches, and workshops with international professionals, attracting a loyal clientele of photographers and photo lovers alike.

🏠 *Via Medardo Rosso 19, 20159*
📞 *+39 02 4548 1569*
URL *www.micamera.com*

"Check the seasonal opening hours on their website. The owners are very kind and would help you find you prints and books and send them to your home."

– Chiara Mirelli

19 Galleria l'Affiche
Map C, P.102

Galleria l'Affiche is a dichotomy in two locations: a warehouse treasure trove on Via Nirone full of piled up paintings, frames, postcards, print and graphics; and the other, on Via Unione, is the formal art gallery with monthly monographic exhibitions of emerging contemporary artists. Start your visit from the shop on Via Nirone for information about what temporary exhibitions may be on, and work your way to Via Unione for the full gallery experience.

🕐 1430-2000 (M), 1000-2000 (Tu-Sa)
🏠 Via Nirone 11, 20123, Via Unione 6, 20123
📞 +39 02 8645 0124
URL www.affiche.it

"*Adriano, who selects the artists, has a very interesting and original viewpoint.*"

– Stefania Beltrame & Paolo Bazzani

20 Teatro Franco Parenti

Map G, P.107

Serving as a true champion of the arts, this creative hub brings a mix of drama, music, concerts, debates, experimental performances and more to its stage. A renovation in 2008 by architect Michele De Lucchi opened the space to span nearly 5,400-square-metre over three levels. Teatro Franco Parenti often hosts the debut performances of the newest Italian and international shows, as well as putting on great classics revisited with a contemporary twist. Consult the programme of events before visiting as many special events as you can. Pop-up flea markets also take place on some weekends.

🏠 *Via Pier Lombardo 14, 20135*
URL *www.teatrofrancoparenti.it*

"Go in the afternoon and wait for a programme to start in the foyer with a glass of wine. The flooring there visually creates a continuous stage."

– Laura Lamonea, Video Sound Art

21 Anteo spazioCinema
Map F, P.106

Home to Milano Design Film Festival, Anteo is renowned for its diverse quality film choices. First opened in 1939 with a single screen, the historic venue now has four screens and an exciting, evolving programme of events on offer. From breakfasts in the cinema to workshops, screenings and film discussion groups, there's a plethora of interesting activities taking place. Between June and mid-September, Anteo hosts an open-air cinema – Arianteo – which shows a variety of films.

S €8.50/6, Weekdays before 1750: €5.50/5
A Via Milazzo 9, 20121
URL www.spaziocinema.info

"It's the most beautiful cinema in Italy and the first multiplex to screen essay films. I also love this place because this is where my first film was shown."

– Marco Pozzi

22 Cinema Beltrade
Map L, P.109

Unknown to even many Milanese people, this small cinema near the Central Railway Station is a secret place for those who are passionate about art films and documentaries. At risk of closure in recent years because of the advent of the multiplexes, the cinema was restyled and saved, affirming its place as an alternative cinema. Interestingly, Beltrade is on Via Nino Oxilia, named after the late Nino Oxilia, a prominent filmmaker from the early 1900s.

🏠 Via Nino Oxilia 10, 20127
📞 +39 02 2682 0592
URL www.bah.hcad.it

"All movies are shown in their original versions with Italian subtitles."
– LaTigre

23 Museo del Design 1880-1980

Map M, P.110

Founded in 1988 by Raffaello Biagetti, the vision for this museum was to exhibit some of the most important and noteworthy designs of the last century. Now home to one of the biggest design collections in Europe, explore the evolution of creativity applied to objects through work of Ettore Sottsass, Le Corbusier, Gio Ponti, Charles and Ray Eames, Eero Saarinen, Arne Jacobsen and many other masters of contemporary design. For an immersive experience, check out the Piccolo Cinema, a collection of video footage featuring many of the designers whose work is on show.

🕐 1030-2000 (Tu, Th-Su), -2100 (W)
💲 €10 🏠 Via Borsi 9, 20143
📞 +39 02 8341 3302
URL www.museiitaliani.org

"The Piccolo Cinema del Design opens till late every Wednesday and often has a happy hour for visitors."

– Alberto Biagetti & Laura Baldassari

24 Pirelli HangarBicocca
Map Q, P.111

Once a factory for manufacturing train car-
riages, the Hangar's days of diesel have been
replaced with creativity. Dedicated to experi-
mentation and research, the expansive venue
lets champions of the contemporary art world
create art in relation to the characterful space.
Aside from the ever-changing schedule of
exhibitions and thoughtful public programmes,
HangarBicocca is also home to sculptures
and paintings by German artist Anselm Kiefer,
including the installation *The Seven Heavenly
Palaces* conceived for its opening. Don't miss
Fausto Melotti's monumental piece perma-
nently installed at the entrance garden.

🕙 1000–2200 (Th–Su) 🏠 Via Chiese 2, 20126
📞 +39 02 6611 1573 URL www.hangarbicocca.org

*"Go there if you want to experience an alternative
museum."*

– Paolo Santambrogio

Markets & Shops

High fashion brands, avant-garde design and handmade curiosities

Food and fashion are synonymous with the Italian shopping experience, and in Milan you'll find definitively more. Marketplaces, both permanent and temporary, are a tradition in town, starting from the open air markets that sell daily sundries and fresh, locally-grown food, to the ones that dedicate to specialised antiquities and vintage clothing. Go to Vecchi Libri in Piazza (*www.piazzadiaz.com*) for second-hand books and first editions, or Via Armorari market for rare coins and stamps. Home to one of the world's biggest fashion events, Milan Fashion Week takes place twice a year, attracting some of the most forward-thinking designers and labels in town. Fashionistas should not miss Quadrilatero della Moda, where the window displays alone are work of art. After that, wander down to the San Babila area for more international and local branded ready-to-wear. For something special to bring home, tour around the smaller concept stores in the Navigli and Brera (#12) neighbourhoods. They are the ideal places to discover emerging designers, original designs and unique finds ranging from photography, home decor, music to stationery.

Giulia Bersani
Photographer & artist

Born in Milan, I mainly work with analogue cameras and create sensitive emotional images. I use photography as a therapy, as a way to keep my past with me and the bad thoughts at bay.

Excelsior Milano
P.054

Olimpia Zagnoli
Illustrator

Born on a leap day in north Italy, Zagnoli now lives in Milan in a house with a kaleidoscopic floor. Lately she's been regularly drawing for The New York Times and La Repubblica.

Luca Finotti
Video director & editor

I'm a communicator. My work starts from the word "idea" and includes fashion films for Giorgio Armani and magazines, featuring stars such as Lady Gaga and Monica Bellucci.

10 Corso Como
P.052

Casa Picone
P.055

SOLO
vinili e libri
P.057

Felix Petruška
Illustrator & animator

Born and based in Milan, I like the polluted, cosy city as it is. Find me strolling around in autumn and winter, and barricaded into my fridge in summer months.

Sarah Mazzetti
Illustrator

A well-recognised illustrator, Sarah Mazzetti draws for clients that include The New York Times and Adobe. She also teaches at IED (Milan) and co-curates for self-publishing brand, Teiera.

Federico Bernocchi
Film critic & radio host

Currently the host of Canicola on Radio 2, Bernocchi also wrote TV show Pechino Express. He founded website "I 400 calci" and contributes to magazines, from Wired to Rivista Studio.

Spazio b**k
P.056

Foto Veneta Ottica
P.058

Lorenzo De Bartolomeis
Co-founder, ddpstudio

After working with Isao Hosoe, he founded ddpstudio with Gabriele Diamanti and Filippo Poli. Since 2014 they have collaborated with Istituto Italiano di Tecnologia on robotics projects for humans.

Spazio Rossana Orlandi
P.060

Tommaso Nani & Noa Ikeuchi, *mist-o*

Established in 2010, mist-o has offices in Milan and Tokyo. Their projects form a bridge between Europe and Asia, spanning from furniture and product, to art direction and interior design.

Emanuele Magini
Industrial & interior designer

I'm also a cook and passionate cyclist. I ran away from my mamma and moved to Milan in 1996 thinking it would be a short stop-over. But then I liked it, and have lived here since.

Fratelli Bonvini
P.059

Nonostante Marras
P.062

Yuval Avital
Composer & multimedia artist

Born in Jerusalem, Avital has a unique voice in the contemporary art scene. His art has appeared in huge sonic events and expands to sound installations, videos and performances.

Mercatone dell' Antiquariato
P.064

Pietro Sedda
Visual artist & tattooist

A trained scenographer, Sedda started tattooing in 1999 from his hometown Oristano to London, Urbino and Milan. He also cooperates with brands and appears in two books published by Logos edizioni.

Andrea Olivo
Photographer

Born in South Africa, I became a photographer of Auraphoto Agency in 2008 and have shot pictures for Vanity Fair and Gioia. I always look for fresh looks and I love this city.

Cargo & HighTech
P.063

East Market
P.065

25 10 Corso Como

Map F, P.106

The famous and fashionable concept store opened by gallerist and publisher Carla Sozzani is situated in an old courtyard in the middle of Corso Como, the shopping district in Milan. A mecca for anything luxury and on-trend, you'll find books, clothes, furniture and magazines in the design shop. There's a café at the entrance with outdoor seating and a gallery with interesting temporary exhibitions, often of renowned photographers. 10 Corso Como also runs a boutique hotel called "3 Rooms". The three suites overlook the lush courtyard and are furnished with the works of 20th century masters like Eero Saarinen and Marcel Breuer.

🕐 1030–2100 (W–Th), –1930 (F–Tu), Restaurant & café: 1100–0100 daily
🏠 Corso Como 10, 20154
📞 +39 02 2900 2674, +39 02 6535 31
URL www.10corsocomo.com
f 10 Corso Como

"Look for the rooftop garden!"
– Giulia Bersani

26 Excelsior Milano
Map C, P.103

Designed by architects Jean Nouvel and Vincenzo de Cotiis, this luxury department store spans seven floors. The spatial design transports you into a world of fashion, perfume, electronics and fine foods through futuristic video installations. Antonia Giacinti, co-owner of the celebrated Antonia boutique in Milan, is in charge of the selection of the brands on the fashion floors, while in the basement the food store is a re-imagined version of a traditional open air market.

🕐 1000–2030 daily, Food store: 1000–2200, Café Excelsior: 0800–2200 🏠 Galleria del Corso 4, 20100 ☎ +39 02 7630 7301 URL www.excelsiormilano.com

"Keep an eye out for the great scenographic installations by Joann Tan, the famous creative director and head architect of Maison Moschino."

– Luca Finotti

27 Casa Picone

Map D, P.104

Giuseppe Picone made history in the 1960s as one of the first ceramist, textile and fashion designer who gave a place to "Made in Italy" in the world with his tailor-made clothes, textiles and craft objects decorated with style and irony. In 2008 Dominique Giroud, Sophie Morichi and Martina Bersani, the heirs of his tradition, brought from Rome to Milan his huge archive and relaunched the brand. Casa Picone is an atelier, a little museum and a shop full of creativity where you can find all kinds of Italian designed treasures.

🏠 Via Nino Bixio 27, 20129
☎ +39 339 7279166
URL casapicone.blogspot.com
✎ By appointment only

"Simply put, this is Marimekko's Italian version."

– Olimpia Zagnoli

28 Spazio b**k
Map K, P.109

More than just a bookstore, Spazio b**k is situated in the bohémien Isola district by two young women, Chiara Bottani and Diletta Colombo. It's a shop and laboratory specialising in illustrated books for kids and adults, from graphic illustrations and comics, independent zines and art books to prints and stationery. The duo organises workshops and events, spanning different fields, all linked by a motto: to see and to make. Look at their website to see the full calendar of events.

🕐 1600–2000 (Su–Tu), 1100–1430, 1600–2000 (W–F), 1100–2000 (Sa)
🏠 Via Porro Lambertenghi 20, 20159
📞 +39 02 8706 3126
🔗 www.spaziobk.com
f Spazio bk

"There's often something nice happening here!"
– Sarah Mazzetti

29 SOLO vinili e libri
Map U, P.111

Focused mainly but not solely on the hipster culture and punk and independent music records, SOLO vinili e libri is one of a kind in the city, where you can find refined research of niche and international products. Whilst vinyls are a main feature of the shop, there's also multitude of comics, fanzines, t-shirts, magazines, books and posters. On occasion, the shop also hosts temporary art and graphic exhibitions.

🕐 1000–1300, 1500–1900 (Tu–F),
1100–1900 (Sa)
🏠 Via Carlo Tenca 10/C, 20124
📞 +39 02 4547 8584
URL www.solovinile.com

"The very kind and helpful owner Pietro Bossi also organises concerts, mainly punk gigs!"

– Federico Bernocchi

30 Foto Veneta Ottica
Map C, P.102

Blink and you might miss this eyewear shop marked only by a sign on the street. With an entrance through the doorway of an ancient building, go up the stairs to the first floor. It's worth the fuss with over 100 years of glasses on display, used and new, with a great variety of prices, styles and offers. Even if you don't need a pair of eye or sunglasses, this shop deserves a visit. Almost all the products come from the private collection of the owner which includes opera glasses and old photo cameras.

🕐 0900–1230, 1500–1920 (M–Sa)
🏠 Via Torino 57, 20123
📞 +39 02 8055 735
URL www.fotovenetaottica.com
f Foto Veneta Ottica occhiali vintage

"*This is an incredible crossover between an optical store and a museum.*"

– Felix Petruška

31 Fratelli Bonvini
Map H, P.107

This old stationery store in the middle of Brera district is great for typography and old graphic enthusiasts. Constructed in 1909, the space was restored in 2014 by a group of friends, maintaining the original furniture, typography machines and tools but giving the space a contemporary and international mood, with temporary exhibitions of artists, workshops and events. Here you can find everything from pencils to books and from collectables to the latest items in design trends.

🕐 1300–1930 (M), 0900– (Tu–Sa)
🏠 Via Tagliamento 1, 20139
📞 +39 02 5392 151
🔗 www.bonvini1909.com
📘 Fratelli Bonvini Milano

"Ask to have a look inside the drawers of the typographic pieces and clichés."

– Lorenzo De Bartolomeis, ddpstudio

32 Spazio Rossana Orlandi
Map B, P.102

Opened in 2002 in a former tie factory, Spazio
Rossana Orlandi is a haven for design lovers,
especially in April during the Milan Design
Week. The namesake founder and entrepreneur is a forecaster and curator of new and
young designers. Her place represents an
unconventional approach to spatial design
mixing a showroom, retail space, offices and
a courtyard with no boundaries between the
different activities. Here you'll find everything
from the most up-to-date limited design
pieces down to smaller home accessories.

🕙 1000–1900 (M-Sa)
🏠 Via Matteo Bandello 14/16, 20123
📞 +39 02 4674 471
URL rossanaorlandi.com
f SPAZIO ROSSANA ORLANDI

"This is a very evocative place for special objects."
– Tommaso Nani & Noa Ikeuchi, mist-o

33 Nonostante Marras
Map N, P.110

Serving as the headquarters of the fashion designer Antonio Marras, this multi-faceted space occupying a ground floor and a basement is a concept store, bookshop, art exhibition venue and office. When you cross the two front doors you enter a secret garden away from the city chaos, and are surrounded by decadentism interiors with the allure of the time. Stop and read a book, visit a temporary exhibition or pick out a dress or an object to buy from a curated selection. To gain entrance, be sure to ring the bell, even twice!

🕐 1000–1900 (Tu–Sa)
🏠 Via Cola di Rienzo 8, 20144
📞 +39 02 7628 0991
URL www.antoniomarras.it

"This is Antonio Marras' kingdom!"

– Emanuele Magini

34 Cargo&HighTech
Map F, P.106

Near the glamourous Corso Como shopping and dining district, this big multi-brand store opened in 1982 and is still avant-garde for its attention to materials and new trends for home interiors. You can find from the gadget, the pen and the detail to clothes collections, home fragrances and big furnitures. In the 17th century, the space an ink factory and ware-house of the newspaper Corriere della Sera and to this day maintains the industrial atmosphere in its many rooms linked by lots of stairs.

🕐 1330-1930 (M), 1030- (Tu-Su)
🏠 Piazza XXV Aprile 12, 20124
📞 +39 02 6241 101
🔗 www.cargomilano.it
📘 Cargo&HighTech

"Everything here is a titbit. If this is not enough, they also have an outlet in the suburbs (via Privata Antonio Meucci 43, 20128)."

– Yuval Avital

35 Mercatone dell'Antiquariato
Map E, P.105

Every last Sunday of the month, over 380 exhibitors from all over Europe sell all kinds of antique items – engravings, clothes, bags, furniture, books and other oddities along the banks of canal Naviglio Grande. A tradition for the Milanese, this famous open-air market starts at around 9am when it is the most crowded and ends at dusk. Be sure to bring cash with you. Also pop into the courtyards that are open to the public on market day and grab a bite at one of the many restaurants and cafés nearby.

🕐 *Monthly last Sundays except Aug & Dec*
🏠 *The Darsena to via Valenza, Naviglio Grande, 20144*
📞 *+39 02 8940 9971*
🔗 *www.navigliogrande.mi.it*

"Visit in the early morning for the best finds, or in the late afternoon for good bargains."

– Pietro Sedda

36 East Market
Map P, P.111

This market has become the place to be on a Sunday, especially for vintage lovers. The exhibitors are all carefully selected and come with original, unique pieces. Set in one of the few remaining old factories that haven't been converted into lofts or showrooms yet, the market is full of character. Stroll through the stands, have breakfast or lunch or have a beer by the DJ mixer. Full of galleries, this area is also known for being the design district of the city.

🕐 1000–2100 (Su)
🏠 Via Privata Giovanni Ventura 14, 20134
📞 +39 392 0430 853
URL www.eastmarketmilano.com
f eastmarketmilano

"The food trucks there are excellent!"
– Andrea Olivo

Carlo e Camilla @ P.070

Restaurants & Cafés

Milanese recipes, diverse regional eats and world-renowned chefs

Everything in Italy happens around a table. And while Milan's fashion industry has been stealing the international spotlight for long, its food scene is catching up – flourishing with chic new restaurants, offering food experience that is as impressive as the unsung local classics. Inheriting the Italian culture of bountiful food and home to a high concentration of Michelin star chefs, Milan will leave an unforgettable taste on your palate. Start the day light with a cappuccino and brioche from a local café. Lunch can be enjoyed on the run by picking up a light bite from Giacomo Tabaccheria (#45) or through a long, indulgent affair at DA NOI IN (#41). Having an Aperitivo before dinner is a must. This quintessential part of the Milanese lifestyle consists of appetising cocktails with a wide variety of food choices ranging from the simple nibbles of olives and fresh mozzarella to a lavish buffet of oysters, fresh salads and pizza that keep your stomach satisfied for the rest of the evening. Dinner is a culturally immersive experience. You won't mind sitting almost back-to-back with other patrons at Latteria San Marco (#43), when you can have a taste of Chef Arturo's homey Milanese cuisine, or even dining at the same table with some 60 guests you've only just met for a taste of chef Carlo Cracco's latest creations (#37). As the Milanese develop a consciousness and curiosity about their food tradition, the creativity that combines traditional recipes reinterpreted offers a truly unique dining experience.

Paride Vitale
Brand & event consultant

My flatmate Ettore is the most beautiful Jack Russell in the world, who's addicted to flying business class and gin tonic. I've been in Milan for 17 years and would only leave it for Tokyo (in allegato).

Giacomo
Pasticceria
P.072

Cristiano Seganfreddo
Founder, Progetto Marzotto

I am a creative entrepreneur, Vice President of Intertrade Group and Agenzia del Contemporaneo. I founded BonottoEditions and am on the Administration Boards of listed companies.

Emanuela Bosone
Singer-songwriter

Under alias Manupuma, I create with many musical influences, especially jazz and electronic music. My first album "Ladruncoli" was released through Universal Records in 2014.

Carlo e
Camilla
P.070

Un posto a
Milano @Cascina Cuccagna
P.073

Matias Perdomo
Chef, Contraste

Contraste is the result of the culinary team's experiences and fantasies – their desire to find harmony between many senses. The proof comes at time of service, so enjoy it!

DA NOI IN
@Magna Pars
Suites Milano
P.076

Paola Manfrin
Founder & director, Luxury Box

As well the creative director of EGO of White, Red & Green; and co-editor of magazine Permanent Food, Manfrin created interviewmatch.it that talks with artists, architects and thinkers.

Porzia Bergamasco
Journalist & curator

Born in Bari and based in Milan for 16 years, I work as a freelance journalist specialising in architecture and design. I also teach Aesthetic at IED and curate for Milano Design Film Festival.

Contraste
P.074

Asso di Fiori
P.077

Consuelo Nocita
CEO & founder, Madeinart

Also an intellectual property lawyer, Nocita is a passionate collector of modern and contemporary Italian art and design. Madeinart is where she produces and diffuses culture and art.

Al Vecchio Aratro P.079

Antonio Aricò
Industrial designer

Passionate about his work and traditional techniques, Aricò (1983) builds his own limited collections and collaborates with brands such as Barilla Group, Seletti and Alessi.

Alessandro Maffioletti
Art director & illustrator

Maffioletti, alias alvvino, studied design at Politecnico and Birmingham Institute of Art and Design. He likes to think that one day he'll be back to seaside where he belongs.

Latteria San Marco P.078

Giacomo Tabaccheria P.080

Maddalena Casadei
Founding partner, Studio Irvine

Marialaura Rossiello and I run Studio Irvine, where we express our love for new challenges and develop art directions for start-ups where we can build a vision.

Ma' Hidden Kitchen Supper Club P.082

The Chic Fish
Blog & creative studio

Built on the passion of Giovanni Gennari and Anna Carbone, The Chic Fish is where graphic, web design, interiors and set design blend, in a style we call "Contemporary Vintage".

Marco Guazzini
Industrial designer

I'm originally from Prato. I have been in Milan for 10 years where I collaborate with design companies and galleries from interiors to object design. My goal is always to innovate.

La Coloniale P.081

U Barba P.083

37 Carlo e Camilla
Map M, P.110

The dining experience at Carlo e Camilla is a symphony of design and culinary excellence, brought by Michelin-starred chef Carlo Cracco, art director Tanja Solci and manager Nicola Fanti. Each night, guests will be treated to finely crafted food in communal seating set with Richard Ginori tableware, inside a raw rustic-looking sawmill. The menu changes often but the focus remains on quality ingredients and recipes that revisit the tradition with innovative techniques. Early booking is recommended, but you can also walk in just for a memorable cocktail.

🕐 1800–0200 daily
🏠 Segheria, Via Giuseppe Meda 24, 20141
📞 +39 02 8373 963
URL www.carloecamillainsegheria.it

"*It's better to arrive before dinner and stay till late for a drink prepared by Filippo, the extraordinary and creative bartender.*"

– Paride Vitale

38 Giacomo Pasticceria

Map D, P.104

Senses awaken in this classic but whimsical pastry shop that rejuvenates every day thanks to the explosion of sweets and colours for the taste buds and the eyes. Journey through inventions of creams and chocolates, surrounded by an old-styled interior, classic and chic in design. Giacomo Pasticceria is a small shop ideal for breakfast or tea time, and enjoy a delicious fruit tart, raspberry millefeuille, brioche or its famous chocolate cakes, like the one with pear.

🕐 0800-2000 daily
🏠 Via Pasquale Sottocorno 5, 20129
📞 +39 02 7631 9147
URL www.giacomopasticceria.com

"Look at the interior full of marble, brass and frescoes. You'll think you were in a contemporary Belle Époque!"

– Cristiano Seganfreddo, Progetto Marzotto

39 Un posto a Milano
@Cascina Cuccagna
Map G, P.107

Built in 1700, Cascina Cuccagna was once an ancient farmstead and is now an oasis in the centre of the city transformed into a cultural and sustainability hub. There's a restaurant inside called Un posto a Milano that serves organic and seasonal food cultivated in small local farms that carry out ethical and sustainable production. Dishes can be enjoyed en plein air or inside, where you can see the magnificent restoration of the building. Un posto a Milano is also a guest house with a limited number of rooms, a cosy location to connect with the local crowd.

🕐 1000-0100 (Tu-Su) 📍 Via Cuccagna 2, 20135 📞 +39 02 5460 061
🔗 www.unpostoamilano.it 📘 un posto a Milano

"Better to make a reservation if you want to dine at the restaurant."

– Emanuela Bosone aka Manupuma

40 Contraste

Map M, P.110

Imagine a restaurant with no menu – that's precisely what Michelin Star chef Matias Perdomo did, alongside two friends, Simon Press, the sous-chef, and Thomas Piras, the maître. Dishes are tailored for each guest according to their desire and complete with fun, surprising elements fuelled by chef's inspiration. There is also a tasting menu with seven courses and a short à la carte menu for those who only desire one to two courses. The location is also unforgettable, set in an intimate space inside an ancient Milanese villa, with a quiet country vibe hidden in the midst of the metropolis chaos.

🕐 1900–2300 (W–M)
🏠 Via Giuseppe Meda 2, 20136
☎ +39 02 4953 6597
URL www.contrastemilano.it
f Contraste Milano

"It's a pit stop for an emotional eating experience. Enjoy it!"

– Matias Perdomo, Contraste

41 DA NOI IN
@Magna Pars Suites Milano
Map E, P.105

With two fireplaces, lots of ancient books, the panorama of a magic garden of lavender outside the windows, the kitchen in view and the menu of Michelin star chef Fulvio Siccardi are the distinguishing features of this fine establishment. The smell and aroma of the herbs fill the air and are infused in the food, which is a creative interpretation of the Italian traditional cuisine. Try the many types of bread – wholemeal cereals, sesame and cheese, poppy seeds and piquillo pepper or the Lingue di Suocera made by artisan bakery Mario Fongo. Bread is served with Tuscan extra virgin olive oil Tenute Argentaia.

🕐 1230–1430, 1930–2230 (M–Sa)
🏠 Via Vincenzo Forcella 6, 20144
📞 +39 02 8338 371
URL www.danoi-in.it

"Their dish with raw amberjack, vegetable brunoise, liquid Grana Padano and truffle is to die for."

– Paola Manfrin, Luxury Box

42 Asso di Fiori
Map E, P.105

A must visit for cheese lovers, this historic restaurant in the Navigli area serves everything from starters to desserts, all with cheese featuring as an ingredient. To add to the theme of cheese, you'll find fake cows everywhere. Quaint in style and size, there are only a few tables which overlook the water of the Naviglio Grande canal, so make sure to book ahead. Taste the Risotto del Contadino with cheese and pears and give Gorgonzola ice cream a try.

🕐 1900-2330 (M-Sa), 1200-1500 (Su, at Mercatone dell'Antiquariato only)
🏠 Via Alzaia Naviglio Grande 54, 20144
📞 +39 02 8940 9415
🔗 www.assodifiori.com
📘 Asso di Fiori

"From starter to dessert, cheese is the protagonist!"
– Porzia Bergamasco

43 Latteria San Marco
Map F, P.106

Located in a small former dairy at the heart of
the city, this warm restaurant of 30 seats was
opened in 1965 by Arturo Maggi. He mainly
cooks his domestic recipes in a silver pan, which
are served by his wife Maria – the ingredients
often come from her own vegetable garden
in the countryside. The menu changes every
day but is very typical Milanese fare. Order the
artichoke tagliolini when in season, meatballs
with mixed sauteed vegetables, or Lampredotto
testaroli, which is Italian cow stomach with the
world's earliest recorded pasta.

🕐 1230–1430, 1930–2200 (M–F)
🏠 Via S. Marco 24, 20121
📞 +39 02 659 7653

"You can't get a reservation so better go before 9pm."

– Consuelo Nocita, Madeinart

44 Al Vecchio Aratro
Map R P.111

Opened years ago as a traditional and affordable Tuscan style restaurant, this establishment is now run by Angela and her husband Mario Vozzo from Calabria, offering a mix of classic dishes from these two Italian regions, both famous worldwide for the great food culture. You'll sense Tuscan and Calabrian vibe not only in the service but also in the housemade recipes made of strong flavours. Enjoy the Tuscan fried vegetables and mozzarella, Abbacchio (lamb) and fresh pappardelle. The patrons are very genuine – loud and happy.

🕐 1200–1500, 1930–2330 (M–F), 1230–1500, 1930–2330 (Sa)

🏠 Via Matteo Maria Boiardo 20, 20127

📞 +39 02 261 9137

📘 Al Vecchio Aratro

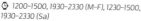

"I suggest trying Gnocchi all'Ortica in Salsa di Noci and ask Angela for the nice stories of her traditions in her dialect!"

– Antonio Aricò

45 **Giacomo Tabaccheria**
Map D, P.104

Hidden near Piazza Cinque Giornate, this small, old-fashioned tobacco shop, café and wine bar is perfect for breakfast as well as after dinner drinks. One of Milan's six Giacomo establishments, the Tabaccheria carries a variety of over 60 products handpicked by the founder Giacomo Bulleri himself. Cold-cuts, pastries from the adjacent Pasticceria (#38), or preserved items like sweet and sour peppers – taste these typical Italian specialties on site, and take some away for later in special packaging. And, of course, you can buy cigarettes.

🕐 0800–2300 daily
🏠 Via Pasquale Sottocorno 5, 20129
📞 +39 02 7600 7948
URL www.giacomotabaccheria.com

"This will be a very special way to begin your day."
– Alessandro Maffioletti aka alvvino

46 La Coloniale
Map E, P.105

This historic wine bar and shop is much loved by an older generation of Milanese people, who come here in the early morning for the first glass of white wine (the traditional Bianchino), while younger generations prefer it for the Aperitivo. There's an excellent selection of wines and champagne, but you can also get cocktails and beers, served on old wooden tables and chairs outside the bar, even in cold evenings. Peruse the food items on sale, including a variety of sweets and salted delicacies, from mushrooms to chocolates and for more you can shop online, in their e-shop.

🕐 0800–2200 (M–Sa), –1930 (Su)
🏠 Corso Genova 19, 20123
📞 +39 02 5810 2346 URL www.lacoloniale.com
f La Coloniale Bottega del Vino

"This is a genuine place where the meeting of different generations is still an advantage."

– Maddalena Casadei, Studio Irvine

47 Ma' Hidden Kitchen Supper Club

This is not a conventional restaurant, it is a private home, and the address is kept secret! There's just one table for eight to ten people, and an ever-changing five course menu inspired by the classic Italian familial dining. Expect to meet new friends, as you may be sharing the table with other diners. The owners – Lele and Elisa – are also the chefs of this fresh new concept and they welcome people through their online reservation system. Alcohol is usually served but BYOB is welcome and free corkage applies.

URL www.mahksc.it
f Ma' Hidden Kitchen Supper Club

"Book in suuuuuper advance! If you're lucky enough to reserve a place at their dinner table, they'll tell you their location by email."

– The Chic Fish

48 U Barba
Map H, P.107

Trendy and authentic, U Barba has become the restaurant of choice for many Milanese, despite the menu being typically Genovan – full of pesto, fish and white meats. This is in part because of the raw post-industrial atmosphere, with its warm refined setting. Ideal for dinner, it is open for lunch sittings but only on the weekends. And if you feel like a night in, you can order online and have the food brought right to your door. Try the Focaccine (flatbread) filled with ingredients of your choice from the menu, or the handmade pasta fresca.

🕑 1900-2300 (Tu-F), 1200-1500, 1900-2300 (Sa-Su)
🏠 Via Pier Candido Decembrio 33, 20137
📞 +39 02 4548 7032
URL www.ubarba.it
f U Barba Osteria Genovese e Bocciofila

"Dine at the nice backyard and try to play a game
at the Bocce court there."

– Marco Guazzini

Nightlife

Street side Aperitivi, frenetic clubbing and artisan cocktails

Milanese nightlife begins after work, around 7pm in a local haunt for an Aperitivo. Like their fellow Italians, the people of Milan love to spend the night outside, literally on the streets, drinking and talking with friends, some even stay until the early hours of the morning. Local's favourite drinks include Negroni (Campari, vermouth and gin) and Spritz (Prosecco, bitter liqueur and sparkling mineral water, topped with an olive or a slice or orange). Part of the crowd would head to nightclubs after Aperitivo, where exciting themes and quality DJ sounds bring the parties to a full swing. Ranging from the seedy and free-spirited to the glamorous and exclusive, one of the most interesting venues is perhaps the infamous Club Plastic (#51). Often nicknamed "the Italian Studio 54", the transgressive and fun nightclub is where you can easily spot international celebrities. For really good live music, you are spoiled for choice. There's Blue Note (#53), a mecca for jazz; Tunnel Club (#49), an alternative music house and Dude Club, featuring an excellent line-up of electronic music, just to name a few. For a quiet and cultured night, opt for the theatre or cinema, which boast world-class performances and diverse screening programmes all year round. Remarkable venues such as Teatro alla Scala mostly concentrated at the very heart of the city, a perfect place to go after an Aperitivo. From rooftop lounges and underground clubs to a simple long drawn out dinner, Milan's vibrant nightlife means there's something for everyone.

Gionata Gesi aka Ozmo
Visual artist

I'm a visual artist. I work with images in various media and pioneer street art in the late 1990s.

Punks Wear Prada
P.090

Vivetta Ponti
Founder, Vivetta

After working at Roberto Cavalli, I created Vivetta in 2009. I love cats (all animals actually), the fifties and sixties, Surrealism, La Nouvelle Vague Anna Karina and collecting old toys.

Silvana Annicchiarico
Director, La Triennale di Milano

As an architect, I've been involved in the fields of research, criticism and teaching. I'm also a member of La Triennale di Milano's Scientific Committee for design, manufacturing and handicraft.

Tunnel Club
P.088

Club Plastic
P.091

Jack Jaselli
Singer, songwriter & producer

I was born in Milan and raised around the world. I love traveling, surfing and reading. I drink too much coffee.

Blue Note
P.093

Beppe Giacobbe
Illustrator

Born in Milan in 1953, Giacobbe studied in New York before returning to his hometown in the 1990s. He contributes regularly to Corriere della Sera and Courrier international next to his personal projects.

Simon Beckerman
Depop, PIG & Retrosuperfuture

Born in 1974, he opened a graphic design studio with his brother Daniel where they launched PIG Mag and eyewear brand, Super. He created app Depop, where people can trade clothes online.

La Salumeria della Musica
P.092

DRY Cocktails & Pizza
P.094

Maria Cristina Didero
Journalist & curator

Didero has worked for Vitra Design Museum and Fondazione Bisazza as Director. She curated an exhibition about the radical design of Studio65 for GAM, Turin, and published *Michele De Lucchi*.

Elita Bar
P.097

Michele Ranauro
Composer & producer

I am a composer, piano virtuoso, producer, "astronaut", an ex-genius now working with genius cows. And I write symphonies if I insist.

studioWOK
Architectural studio

Set up by Marcello Bondavalli, Nicola Brenna and Carlo Alberto Tagliabue, studioWOK researches into architecture, landscape and sustainability, questing quality living and public space.

The Botanical Club
P.096

Frida
P.098

Atelier VM
Jeweller

Founded in 1998 by Marta Cafarelli and Viola Naj Oleari, Atelier VM is a gold jewellery brand and alchemic workshop. We design essential and poetic jewels for everyday life.

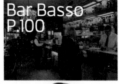

Bar Basso
P.100

Luisa Bertoldo
PR entrepreneur

I manage communication strategies for stories and projects from fashion to food. I live with my family on a building's top where I can listen to the city's buzz while watching the snowy mountain tops.

Alessandra & Francesca Minini, *Gallerists*

We run a contemporary art gallery in the Ventura Lambrate district, and travel a lot for work. Milan became our home, and we are always open to try everything is new in town!

Tongs Bar
P.099

Cantine Isola
P.101

49 Tunnel Club
Map L, P.109

In addition to the good concerts and DJ mixes, the Tunnel Club is a must-see for its unique and unusual location: in a real tunnel built below the Central Station's rails. Tunnel Club is an amazing place for lovers of electronic sounds, indie rock, hip hop concerts and more niche live music shows. Django Django, Taylor Davis and Mathew Jonson are a few of the many talented and international artists to have recently played here.

🕐 💲 *Showtime & admission vary with programmes* 🏠 *Via Giovanni Battista Sammartini 30, 20125* 📞 *+39 339 4032 702* 📘 *Tunnel Club*

"Nice club, DJ and live music."
– Gionata Gesi aka Ozmo

50 Punks Wear Prada (PWP)

Punks Wear Prada (PWP) is a Friday night party founded by fashionista Natasha Slater. Dance to pop and electronic music rendered by international DJs amongst glammed up fashion junkies, posers, models and hipsters. Be prepared to go all out with what you wear – weird and wonderful eccentricism is the way to fit in with the fluorescent and psychedelic decor in PWP parties of diverse themes. Check its facebook page for updated venue and occasional crossover events with fashion brands.

🕐 2300–0400 (F)
💲🏠 Admission & venue vary with parties
📞 +39 338 9733 224
URL natashaslater.com/events
f PWP

"*Experience one of the most fashionable and fun nights in Milan.*"

– Vivetta Ponti, Vivetta

51 Club Plastic
Map I, P.108

A lineup of stars including Andy Warhol, Keith Haring and Madonna have graced the stage here. Set in a post-industrial space with a private mezzanine and plush sitting area, this iconic and worldwide renowned Milanese club from the 1980s is run by Lucio Nisi and Nicola Guiducci. The club is popular among young crowds on Friday night, while Saturdays are packed with fans of the Club Domani theme and on Sundays, those enjoy live entertainment. With its aura of coolness, the club welcomes the daringly and glamorously dressed. Nonetheless, a selective door policy is maintained so it is best to prepare a back-up plan for the night.

🕐 2300–0500 (F), 2345– (Sa), 2300–0300 (Su)
🏠 Via Gargano 15, 20139
📘 Club Plastic - Milano

"It's one of the most iconic and crazy club to dance in."
– Silvana Annicchiarico, La Triennale di Milano

52 La Salumeria della Musica
Map I, P.108

Once a gold manufacturing space, now a massive haven for music lovers, La Salumeria della Musica is also a delicatessen! Machinery and other artefacts of the venue's manufacturing heritage remain, adding character to the live concerts hosted here. Expect all kinds of musical performances from rock, funk, soul, jazz, pop and more, all accompanied by good wine and a fine selection of cured meats. Try the traditional Italian Tagliere – a cutting board full of slices of cured meats, vegetables and cheese.

🕐 💲 Showtime & admission vary with programmes
🏠 Via Antonio Pasinetti 4, 20141
📞 +39 02 5680 7350
URL www.lasalumeriadellamusica.com
f La Salumeria della Musica

"If you're into live music, this mid-size club is an absolute guarantee."

– Jack Jaselli

53 Blue Note
Map K, P.109

Hailed as the mecca of jazz, this is Italy's version of the famous Blue Note Jazz Club of the Greenwich Village in New York. Opened in 2003 in the thriving Isola district, it has hosted the best musicians including Dee Dee Bridgewater, Billy Cobham, Chick Corea, Raphael Gualazzi and Wynton Marsalis. Enjoy good music whilst dining or drinking some of the excellent wine selection. Open six nights a week, the club has at least one show per night at 9pm. Check online for other showtimes and make a booking in advance.

🕐 *1930-0000 (Tu-Su, Sept-May)*
💲 *Admission varies with programmes*
🏠 *Via Pietro Borsieri 37, 20159*
📞 *+39 02 6901 6888*
🔗 *www.bluenotemilano.com*

"Go there for excellent jazz, taste good food or just a drink."

– Beppe Giacobbe

54 DRY Cocktails & Pizza
Map F, P.106

There are many reasons to stop into this new modern cocktail bar in the centre of the city. The concept was created by renowned chef Andrea Berton and his talented team. The bartender, Guglielmo Miriello from the Sugar Bar at Maison Pourcel in Shanghai prepares vintage and forgotten cocktails as well as regular classics. The minimalist design by architect Tiziano Vudafieri makes for a relaxing experience, and the menu has both traditional pizzas and a wide selection of innovative "Pizze dello Chef" that can be customised with fresh condiments served at the table.

🕐 1900–0130 daily, Pizzeria: –0000
🏠 Via Solferino 33, 20121
📞 +39 02 6379 3414
URL www.drymilano.it

"Needless to say, the cocktails are amongst the best in the city. And the pizzas are creative too."

– Simon Beckerman, Depop, PIG & Retrosuperfuture

55 The Botanical Club
Map K, P.109

What began as an experiment in the Isola district has earned its place as Italy's first small batch gin distillery in 2015. In addition to unusual and sophisticated cocktails, The Botanical Club also offers a fine dining experience, with an experimental and ever-changing menu. The small dishes are designed to be shared so order a few between friends. Building on the success of the club, a second Botanical Club located on Via Tortona 33 has opened. It is great for brunch during the day, with the same fantastic cocktails.

🕐 1930–0200 (M-Sa), Kitchen: ~2330
🏠 Via Pastrengo 11, 20159
📞 +39 02 3652 3846
URL www.thebotanicalclub.com
f The Botanical Club

"Perfect for a drink in the late evening, especially gin cocktails."

– Maria Cristina Didero

56 Elita Bar

Map E, P.105

Initiated by the team behind project Elita, a cultural association known for its parties and mix of music and art, Elita Bar serves some of the best cocktails in town. The eccentric and varied music, casual unpretentious atmosphere and location by the canals are what draw the crowds here at night. Try the Calindri Spritz or a classic gin and tonic, prepared with one of the 30 kinds of gin on hand and the iced nitrogen, designed to keep cocktails at their coldest.

🕐 1700–0200 daily
🏠 Via Corsico 5, 20144
📞 +39 02 3679 8711
URL www.elita.it
f ElitaBAR

"*The former singer of Italian ska band Casino Royale will take you on a journey filled with passion, zesty food, nice music and drinks. Have a walk there, mate!*"

– Michele Ranauro

57 Frida
Map K, P.109

One of the first pubs opened in the recently famous Isola district, now full of restaurants, pubs and little shops, Frida remains the favourite for many. As the end of the week approaches, it's full of people enjoying themselves inside or outside in the big and green courtyard from Aperitivo till late, so it's best to book a table. Pop in during the day to have a cup of tea seated on the comfortable vintage sofas, or for the Sunday brunch. Frida has also a nice vintage shop called Particelle Complementari.

🕐 1000–1500, 1800–0200 (M–F), 1800– (Sa), 1200–0100 (Su)
🏠 Via Antonio Pollaiuolo 3, 20159
📞 +39 02 6802 60
📘 Frida Isola 🌐 www.fridaisola.it

"Let's challenge the seasons and have a drink in the beautiful portico outside."

– studioWOK

58 Tongs Bar

Map E, P.105

Channel the style of the Milanese by drinking beers and talking with friends outside this pub. Popular especially from Aperitivo because of the rich buffet offering, Tongs Bar also runs regular promotions, drawing in crowds for craft beers on tap and large cocktails, especially the signature black Mojito. Inside the pub there's a huge selection of books, facilitating deep and interesting literary conversations and books swapping amongst its guests.

🕐 1800-0200 (Tu-Th), -0300 (F-Sa), 0100 (Su)
🏠 Via Vigevano 19, 20144
📞 +39 347 7042 891
f Tongs Bar Milano

"Here the tradition is to talk with your friends and drink a beer just outside the pub in the middle of the Milanese crowd!"

– Atelier VM

59 **Bar Basso**
Map T, P.111

A haunt for design legends, especially during the city's prominent events such as Milan Design Week and Milan Furniture Fair, Bar Basso is best enjoyed in the evenings for its typical Milanese Aperitivo between 7–9pm. The bar's current cocktail list carries more than 500 drinks ranging from absolute classics to new creations. The famous cocktail Negroni Sbagliato was invented here in the 1960s, a lighter version of the classic Negroni. And for the adventurous, answer "Bicchierone" when the waitstaff ask about the size of your cocktail. The interior is frozen in the 1970s, oozing a cool, retro atmosphere.

🕘 0900–0115 (Tu-Su)
🏠 Via Plinio 39, 20133   📞 +39 02 2940 0580
🔗 Barbasso.com   f Bar Basso

"If you are in Milan during the Design Week, this is the place to go."
– Luisa Bertoldo

60 Cantine Isola
Map J, P.108

This quaint and intimate wine bar and shop near the Isola district is an institution in Milan, with its excellent selection of bottles, especially Italians. Owner of the bar is the Sarais family. They are very helpful in the selection of wine, often encouraging the tasting of smaller independent wines. The crowds start to appear in the late afternoon as the meeting point for locals. In the summer months, enjoy your wine outside on the small patio or directly seated on the sidewalk!

🕐 1000–2200 (Tu–Su)
🏠 Via Paolo Sarpi 30, 20154
📞 +39 02 3315 249
📘 Le Cantine Isola

"Trust the owner's advice on the kind of wine you should taste."

– Alessandra & Francesca Minini

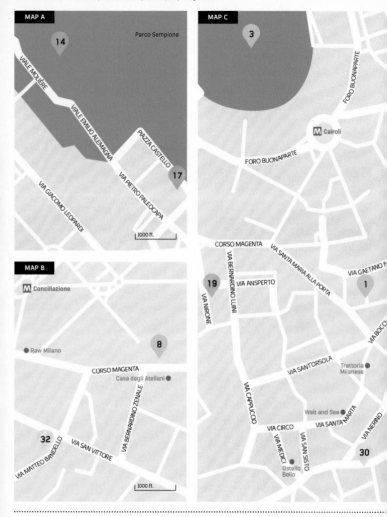

- 1_Piazza degli Affari e L.O.V.E.
- 3_Castello Sforzesco
- 8_Basilica di Santa Maria delle Grazie
- 14_La Triennale di Milano
- 17_Studio Museo Achille Castiglioni
- 19_Galleria l'Affiche
- 30_Foto Veneta Ottica
- 32_Spazio Rossana Orlandi

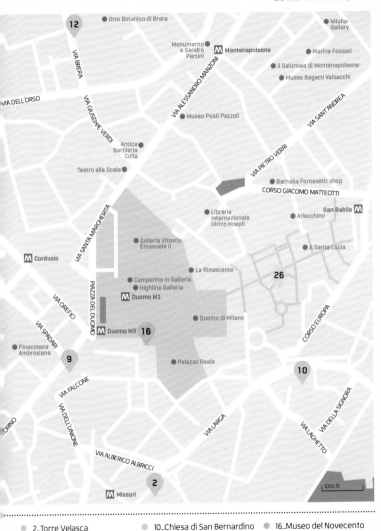

- 2_Torre Velasca
- 9_Chiesa di Santa Maria presso San Satiro
- 10_Chiesa di San Bernardino alle Ossa
- 12_Brera
- 16_Museo del Novecento
- 26_Excelsior Milano

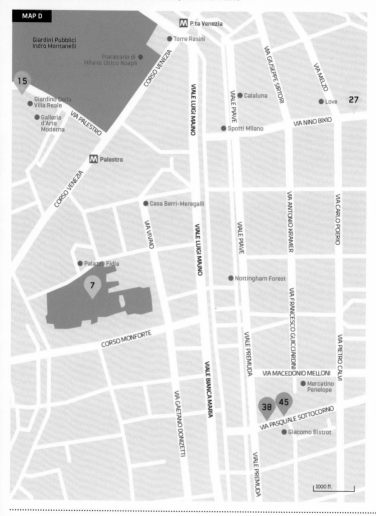

MAP D

Giardini Pubblici Indro Montanelli

M P.ta Venezia

Torre Rasini

Pianetario di Milano Ulrico Hoepli

CORSO VENEZIA

15

Giardino Della Villa Reale

Galleria d'Arte Moderna

VIA PALESTRO

VIALE LUIGI MAJNO

VIALE PIAVE

Calaluna

VIA GIUSEPPE SIRTORI

VIA MELZO

Love

27

Spotti Milano

VIA NINO BIXIO

M Palestro

CORSO VENEZIA

Casa Berri-Meregalli

VIA VIVAIO

VIALE LUIGI MAJNO

VIALE PIAVE

VIA ANTONIO KRAMER

VIA CARLO POERIO

Palazzo Fidia

7

Nottingham Forest

VIA FRANCESCO GUICCIARDINI

CORSO MONFORTE

VIALE PREMUDA

VIA PIETRO CALVI

VIALE BIANCA MARIA

VIA MACEDONIO MELLONI

Mercatino Penelope

VIA GAETANO DONIZETTI

38 45

VIA PASQUALE SOTTOCORNO

Giacomo Bistrot

VIALE PREMUDA

1000 ft.

....

- 7_Villa Necchi Campiglio
- 15_Padiglione d'Arte Contemporanea
- 27_Casa Picone
- 38_Giacomo Pasticceria
- 45_Giacomo Tabaccheria

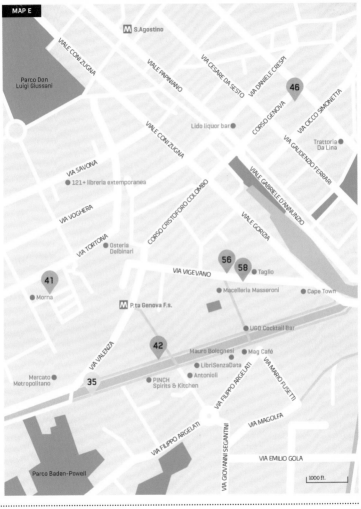

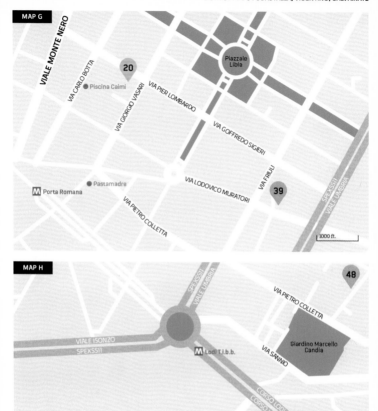

- 13_Fondazione Prada
- 20_Teatro Franco Parenti
- 31_Fratelli Bonvini
- 39_Un posto a Milano
- 48_U Barba

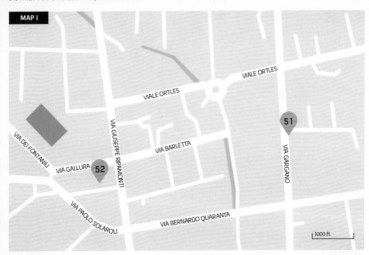

- 5_Casa Rustici
- 51_Club Plastic
- 52_La Salumeria della Musica
- 60_Cantine Isola

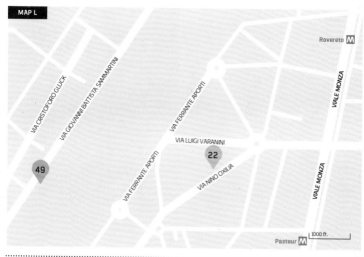

- 18_Micamera
- 22_Cinema Beltrade
- 28_Spazio b**k
- 49_Tunnel Club
- 53_Blue Note
- 55_The Botanical Club
- 57_Frida

DISTRICT MAPS : **MORIVIONE, ZONA SOLARI, PORTA VOLTA**

MAP M

MAP N

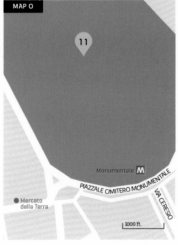

MAP O

- 11_Cimitero Monumentale
- 23_Museo del Design 1880–1980
- 33_Nonostante Marras
- 37_Carlo e Camilla
- 40_Contraste

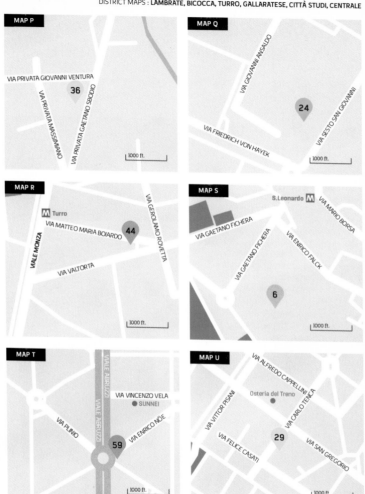

MAP P

VIA PRIVATA GIOVANNI VENTURA
VIA PRIVATA MASSIMIANO
VIA PRIVATA GAETANO SBODIO
36
1000 ft.

MAP Q

VIA GIOVANNI ANSALDO
VIA SESTO SAN GIOVANNI
24
VIA FRIEDRICH VON HAYEK
1000 ft.

MAP R

🚇 Turro
VIALE MONZA
VIA MATTEO MARIA BOIARDO
VIA GEROLAMO ROVETTA
44
VIA VALTORTA
1000 ft.

MAP S

S.Leonardo 🚇 VIA MARIO BORSA
VIA GAETANO FICHERA
VIA GAETANO FICHERA
VIA ENRICO FALCK
6
1000 ft.

MAP T

VIALE ABRUZZI
VIA VINCENZO VELA
● SUNNEI
VIA PLINIO
VIA ENRICO NOE
59
1000 ft.

MAP U

VIA ALFREDO CAPPELLINI
VIA VITTOR PISANI
Osteria del Treno
VIA CARLO TENCA
VIA FELICE CASATI
29
VIA SAN GREGORIO
1000 ft.
Pavè ●

● 6_Complesso abitativo
Monte Amiata

● 24_Pirelli HangarBicocca

● 29_SOLO vinili e libri

● 36_East Market

● 44_Al Vecchio Aratro

● 59_Bar Basso

Accommodation

Hip hostels, fully-equipped apartments & swanky hotels

No journey is perfect without a good night's sleep to recharge. Whether you're backpacking or on a business trip, our picks combine top quality and convenience, whatever your budget.

⬤ <€100 💰 €101–250 💵 >€251+

Palazzo Segreti

Just steps away from Castello Sforzesco and Cairoli metro station, Palazzo Segreti combines convenience and comfort at an unbeatable downtown location with a simple focus on quality living. That tenet runs from its organic breakfast choices to the handmade bath products and smart room designs. Double rooms often feature combined bedroom and bathroom. Some suites have balconies.

🏠 Via San Tomaso, 8, 20121
📞 +39 02 4952 9250 URL palazzosegreti.com 💵

Room Mate Guilia

The promise of a home-like stay sustains with Patricia Urquiola's design and it being a member of the Room Mate group. Inside the 19th century building is a modernised interior, reflecting traits of Milanese love of art and classic Italian domestic setting across its materials and the 85 rooms. Its proximity to transfer station Duomo and free citywide WiFi network are an added bonus.

🏠 Via Silvio Pellico 4 20121   📞 +39 02 8088 8900   💰
URL room-matehotels.com/en/giulia   💲

Armani Hotel Milano

🏠 Via Manzoni, 31, 20121
📞 +39 02 8883 8888
URL milan.armanihotels.com

Senato Hotel Milano

🏠 Via Senato, 22, 20121
📞 +39 02 781 236
URL senatohotelmilano.it

Bed and Breakfast di Porta Tosa

🏠 *Via Annibale Grasselli 11, 20137*
📞 *+39 02 3954 6503*
URL *www.portatosa.it*

ApArt Hotel Lupetta 5

🏠 *Via Lupetta 5, 20123*
📞 *+39 02 8363 1712*
URL *www.aparthotellupetta5.com*

Ostello Bello Medici

🏠 *Via Medici, 4, 20123*
📞 *+39 02 3658 2720*
URL *www.ostellobello.com*

Notes

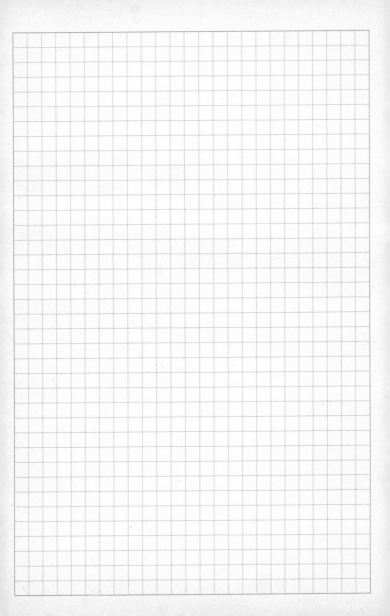

Index

Architecture & Interior

Paolo Bazzani & Stefania Beltrame, p040
www.paolobazzani.it,

studioWOK, p098
www.studiowok.com
Portrait by Federico Villa

Ugo La Pietra, p036
www.ugolapietra.com

Art & Illustration

Beppe Giacobbe, p093
www.beppegiacobbe.com

dotdotdot, p038
dotdotdot.it

Felix Petruška, p058
www.felixpetruska.com

Gionata Gesi aka Ozmo, p088
www.ozmo.it

Goldschmied & Chiari, p022
www.goldiechiari.com
Portrait by Toni Thorimbert

Marco Klefisch, p019
www.marcoklefisch.com
Portrait by Carlo Beccalli

Olimpia Zagnoli, p055
www.olimpiazagnoli.com

Sarah Mazzetti, p056
www.sarahmazzetti.com

Thomas De Falco, p034
thomasdefalco.blogspot.hk

Branding & Advertising

Paride Vitale, p070
www.paridevitale.com
Portrait by Toiletpaper

Culture

Alessandra & Francesca Minini, p101
www.francescaminini.it

Consuelo Nocita @Madeinart, p078
madeinart.it

Cristiano Seganfreddo @Progetto Marzotto, p072
www.progettomarzotto.org

Massimo Torrigiani @Boiler Corporation, p035
www.boilercorporation.com

Nicola Ricciardi, p016
nicolaricciardi.com

Silvana Annicchiarico @La Triennale di Milano, p091
triennale.org

Fashion

Arthur Arbesser @Iceberg, p015
www.arthurarbesser.com
Portrait by Rafael Y. Herman

Atelier VM, p099
www.ateliervm.com

Luisa Bertoldo, p100
luisabertoldo.com
Portrait by Andrea Colzani

Narguess Hatami @Miahatami, p032
www.miahatami.com

Paolo Santambrogio, p046
www.paolosantambrogio.com

Pietro Sedda, p064
www.pietrosedda.com

Simon Beckerman @Depop, PIG & Retrosuperfuture, p094
FB: pigmag, www.depop.com

Vivetta Ponti @Vivetta, p090
www.vivetta.it

Luca Finotti, p054
www.lucafinotti.com

Enrico Pompili , p023
studiovaen.tumblr.com

Film

Federico Bernocchi, p057
www.canicola.rai.it

Marco Pozzi, p042
www.marcopozzi.com

Porzia Bergamasco, p077
www.milanodesignfilmfestival.com
Portrait by Alessandro Zoboli

Food

Matias Perdomo @Contraste, p074
www.contrastemilano.it

Graphics

Alessandro Maffioletti aka alvvino, p080
www.alvvino.org

LaTigre, p043
latigre.net

Laura Lamonea @Video Sound Art festival, p041
www.videosoundart.com

Matteo Morelli, p026
www.matteomorelli.net

Industrial

Alberto Biagetti & Laura Baldassari, p044
atelierbiagetti.com

Antonio Aricò, p079
www.antonioarico.com
Portrait by PEPE fotografia

Damiano Spelta, p017
www.damianospelta.com

Diego Grandi @DGO, p014
www.diegograndi.it
Portrait by Helenio Barbetta

Emanuele Magini, p062
www.emanuelemagini.it

Lorenzo De Bartolomeis @ddpstudio, p059
www.lorenzodebartolomeis.com

Maddalena Casadei @Studio Irvine, p081
www.studio-irvine.com

Marco Guazzini, p083
www.marcoguazzini.com

Nicolas Bellavance-Lecompte, p025
www.nb-lecompte.com

Studio Pepe, p018
www.studiopepe.info
Portrait by Andrea Ferrari

The Chic Fish, p082
www.thechicfish.com

Tommaso Nani & Noa Ikeuchi @mist-o, p060
www.mist-o.com

Music

Emanuela Bosone aka Manupuma, p073
FB: manupumaofficial

Jack Jaselli, *p092*
www.jackjaselli.com

Michele Ranauro, *p097*
FB: ranauromichele

Yuval Avital, *p063*
www.yuvalavital.com

Performing arts

Umberto Angelini
@Uovo, *p024*
www.uovoproject.it
www.uovokids.it
Portrait by Marco Descalzi

Photography

Andrea Olivo, *p065*
www.andreaolivo.com

Chiara Mirelli, *p039*
www.chiaramirelli.com

Giulia Bersani, *p052*
www.giuliabersani.com

Lady Tarin, *p020*
http://ladytarin.com/

Publishing

Maria Cristina Didero, *p096*
Linkedin: Maria Cristina Didero
Portrait by Girgio Possenti

Paola Manfrin
@Luxury Box, *p076*
Pinterest: egoofwrg
Portrait by Carlo Di Pasquale @
ZEPstudio

Photo & other credits

10 Corso Como, *p052-53*
(All) 10 Corso Como

Blue Note, *p093*
(All) Blue Note, Ilaria Pretto

Brera, *p026-027*
(p026) Brera

Carlo e Camilla, *p070-071*
(All) Carlo e Camilla, Chico
Photographer, Enrico De Luigi

Casa Picone, *p055*
(Top) Casa Picone

Contraste, *p074-075*
(p074 All, p075 bottom) Contraste

DA NOI IN @Magna Pars Suites
Milano, *p076*
(Top) DA NOI IN @Magna Pars
Suites Milano

DRY Cocktails & Pizza,
p094-095
(All) DRY Cocktails & Pizza
(p094 Top, p095 middle right, bottom right) Diego Rigatti
(p094 Bottom, p095 top) Santi Cale-
ca (p095 middle left) PEEP HOLE
(bottom left) Simone Lombardi

East Market, *p065*
(All) East Market

Excelsior Milano, *p054*
(All) Excelsior Milano

Foto Veneta Ottica, *p058*
(Middle, bottom) Foto Veneta Ottica

Frida, *p098*
(Bottom left) Frida

Galleria l'Affiche, *p040*
Courtesy of Galleria l'Affiche
(Middle) dell'Unione 6, Federico
Guerri 2016 (bottom) Nirone 11

Giacomo Pasticceria, *p072*
(All) Giacomo Pasticceria
(Left) Hugh Findletar (right)
Gianmarco Grimaldi

Giacomo Tabaccheria, *p080*
(Bottom) Giacomo Tabaccheria,
Cristina Galliena

La Triennale di Milano, *p034*
(Exterior) La Triennale di Milano,
Masiar Pasquali

Padiglione d'Arte
Contemporanea, *p035*
Courtesy of PAC, Padiglione d'Arte
Contemporanea (Middle) Guido
Cataldo (bottom) Zhan Huan

Ma' Hidden Kitchen Supper
Club, *p082*
(All) Dennis Valle

Micamera, *p039*
(Bottom left & right) Micamera,
Pino Musi

Museo del Design 1880-1980,
p044-045
Courtesy of Museo del Design
1880-1980 (p044 Bottom) Charlotte
Hosmer (p045 Bottom) Delfino
Sisto Legnani, Marco Cappelletti

Museo del Novecento,
p036-037

(All) Museo del Novecento,
Comune di Milano – tutti i diritti
di legge riservati
(p036 Top) Thomas Pagani

Nonostante Marras, *p062*
(Middle, bottom) Nonostante
Marras

Piazza degli Affari e L.O.V.E.,
p014
(Bottom) Piazza degli Affari e
L.O.V.E., © Antinori

Pirelli HangarBicocca, *p046-047*
(All) Pirelli HangarBicocca
(p046 Top, middle) Lorenzo Palm-
ieri (p046 Bottom, p047 All) © Attilio
Maranzano (p046 Bottom, p047
top right) dell'artista (p047 top left,
bottom left & right) Carsten Höller
(top right) Gagosian Gallery

Punks Wear Prada, *p090*
(Middle) Punks Wear Prada

Spazio b**k, *p056*
(Bottom) Spazio b**k

Spazio Rossana Orlandi,
p060-061
(p060 Top, middle, p061 top,
middle, bottom left) Spazio Rossana Orlandi

Teatro Franco Parenti, *p041*
(Top, blue house, red house)
Teatro Franco Parenti

The Botanical Club, *p096*
(All) The Botanical Club

Torre Velasca, *p015*
(Bottom) Torre Velasca, © CEpho-
to, Uwe Aranas / CC-BY-SA-3.0

Tunnel Club, *p088-089*
Courtesy of Tunnel Club
(p088 Bottom) Luca Panegatti
(p089 Top left) Fiamma Orco
Tebaldi (top right, bottom) Tunnel Club

Villa Necchi Campiglio,
p020-021
(All) Villa Necchi Campiglio,
Property of FAI - Fondo Ambiente
Italiano (The National Trust for
Italy) since 2001 (p020 Top)
Gabriele Basilico 2015 (p020 Pool,
p021 top) Giorgio Majno 2008 (p021
Green sofa, fireplace) arenaim-
magini.it 2014 (hallway, bottom
right) Massimo Ripani 2009

-
In Accommodation: all courtesy
of respective hotels.

CITIX60

CITIx60: Milan

First published and distributed by
viction workshop ltd

viction:ary™

7C Seabright Plaza, 9–23 Shell Street,
North Point, Hong Kong

Url: www.victionary.com
Email: we@victionary.com
🅕 www.facebook.com/victionworkshop
🐦 www.twitter.com/victionary_
🐱 www.weibo.com/victionary

Edited and produced by viction:ary

Concept & art direction: Victor Cheung
Research & editorial: Queenie Ho, Caroline Kong
Project coordination: Jovan Lip, Katherine Wong
Design & map illustration: MW Wong, Frank Lo

Co-curator & contributing writer: Valentina Raggi
Contributing editor: Katee Hui
Cover map illustration: Federica Ubaldo
Count to 10 illustrations: Guillaume Kashima aka Funny Fun
Photography: Arturo Di Casola

Content is compiled based on facts available as of June 2016. Travellers are
advised to check for updates from respective locations before your visit.

First edition
ISBN 978-988-13204-6-9
Printed and bound in China

Acknowledgements

A special thank you to all creatives, photographer(s), editor, producers, companies and organisations for your crucial contributions to our inspiration and
knowledge necessary for the creation of this book. And, to the many whose
names are not credited but have participated in the completion of the book,
we thank you for your input and continuous support all along.